Interpreting Lucian Freud

Interpreting Lucian Freud

DAVID ALAN MELLOR

TATE PUBLISHING

The exhibition at Tate Britain is sponsored by

�֎ UBS Warburg

Published to accompany the exhibition
at Tate Britain, London
20 June – 22 September 2002
and touring to
Fundació "la Caixa", Barcelona
22 October 2002–12 January 2003
The Museum of Contemporary Art, Los Angeles
9 February–25 May 2003

First published 2002 by order of the Tate Trustees
by Tate Publishing, a division of Tate Enterprises Ltd,
Millbank, London SW1P 4RG
www.tate.org.uk

British Library cataloguing in publication data
A catalogue record for this book is available from
the British Library

ISBN 1 85437 442 7

Distributed in North and South America by
Harry N. Abrams, Inc., New York, under the following ISBN:
ISBN 0 8109 6269 1

Designed by Philip Lewis
Printed in Italy

Dimensions are in centimetres, height before width,
followed by inches in brackets

Front cover: *Large Interior W11 (after Watteau)* 1981–3 (fig.19)
Back cover: *Man's Head (Self-Portrait III)* 1963 (fig.38)
Frontispiece: *Pluto and the Bateman Sisters* 1996 Oil on canvas
175 × 135 (68 7/8 × 15 3/8) Colección Cisneros

Contents

Introduction

Rather than laying out a chronology or history, this book sketches a series of views, some familiar, some unfamiliar, around Lucian Freud and his art. It looks at his concepts of vision, his representations of the human body, and finally at the historical and cultural contexts for his practice as a painter. His themes will be shown to be embedded within the larger cultures of the twentieth century and before.

These analytical sequences begin with a section discussing the forms and style of Freud's distinctive close observation, especially in relation to the play of mirrors and anamorphic distortions. A second section turns to the ways in which this Naturalistic intimacy has produced images of human bodies that challenge notions of a stable, equilibrated existence. The setting for this anti-pastoral – the arena and location for Freud's subjects – is the topic of the third section: the grotesque post-war metropolis, whose dislocations inform the imagination of associated writers such as William Sansom and Rose Macauley. The narrative then moves in a fourth part from this cultural and historical setting to an extraordinary body inhabiting this urban landscape: the monumental and carnivalesque figure of the performance artist Leigh Bowery. Reflections on corporeality form the final section. The sobriety of close and compulsive observation that gives priority to the eye is returned to, concluding with an account of the poetics of paint as skin and skin as paint.

1
Naked Portrait 1972–3
Oil on canvas
61 × 61 (24 × 24)
Tate. Purchased 1975

Forms of Surveillance

After more than sixty years, Lucian Freud's figurative art has developed through a trajectory from the poetic Neo-Romanticism of the 1940s to its current monumental allegories of Realism. A major thread in this transformation has been the complex identity of Freud's Naturalism and its linkages to some of the pictorial forms through which Realism has mutated during the last century or more. One crucial aspect in the Modernist re-definition of Realism – which took place from Edgar Degas to George Grosz – was an abrasive, anti-sentimentalising objectivity.

When Freud reported to William Feaver in a radio interview, *a propos* his human sitters: 'I'm interested, really interested in them as animals',[1] he echoed Degas' investigative Naturalism of the 'human animal'. Just as stylised versions of Grosz's work were extant in British art by the close of the 1930s, so Degas' keyhole observations of the human animal had been domesticated by Walter Sickert since the late 1880s. The manifold cultural cross-currents of the British 1930s and 1940s – of Documentarianism and Mass Observation – emphasised Neo-Realist forensics. By the time of Freud's first published statement, in *Encounter* 1954, the currency of visual regimes of surveillance was well established. Freud metaphorised this pictorial strategy with a figure of constrained interrogation, a trope from the Existentialist imagination in the mid-century Age of Anxiety, where the sitter possessed secrets that must be prised out: 'The subject must be kept under closest observation: if this is done, day and night, the subject – he, she or it – will eventually reveal the all without which selection itself is not possible.'[2] By 1960 this culture of surveillance portrayal had filtered through to popular culture in such TV programmes as the BBC's 'Face to Face', where a media Grand Inquisitor – John Freeman – interviewed public personalities and the camera held their faces in a protracted and overwhelming gaze of interrogative intimacy.

2
Girl with a Kitten 1947
Oil on canvas
39.4 × 29.5 (15 1/2 × 11 5/8)
Private Collection

Sir John Rothenstein has written about the ability of one's own eye compulsively to see more through the agency of Freud's painting:

> The fascinated, unblinking stare with which Lucian Freud fixed his subjects enabled him to represent them in a manner that makes it impossible for the spectator (for this spectator at least) ever to look at them casually: the eye is compelled to see them, down to the smallest detail, with something of the intensity with which he saw them himself.[3]

It was Sigmund Freud, Lucian's grandfather, who had identified as early as 1905 the compelling drive to see, terming it 'scopophilia'. In *Three Essays on Sexuality* he linked the 'pleasure of looking' at the (naked) body with the sense of tactile experience, so that sight and corporeality came together on a field of desire.[4] As Lucian Freud has said regarding his transcription of his sight of the nude: 'part of liking to work from them naked is that I can see more.'[5]

As well as such personal drives, there was the issue of the larger imaginary universe of the mid-century – which both politically and socially was replete with hidden secrets and private duress. When, in 1963, Freud made another short statement in *Cambridge Opinion*,[6] it was clearly under the shadow of Cold War exterminism, but it centred, as in 1954, on the illuminating omnipotence of the artist in the face of the nuclear event horizon: 'this new dimension, having the end in sight can give the artist supreme control, daring and such an awareness of his bearings in existence that he will (in Nietzsche's words) create conditions under which "a thousand secrets of the past crawl out of their hiding places – into his sun"'.[7] What was also disclosed by this short text was Freud's drive to absolute clarification. In his paintings this was manifest in his wish to re-organise the spectacle of the human body in order to bring things to light, to disclose desire in light – sometimes the cold north light and sometimes the glare of the 500-watt electric bulb. He represented this revelatory malleability of the depicted body under his gaze to William Feaver: 'I might use something which would actually be visible from another position because it's something that I like that I would show in light.'[8] Here, perhaps, was one of the foundational tropes of Western art – the disclosing gesture of light on the body in

3
Sunny Morning – Eight Legs
1997
Oil on canvas
234 × 132.1 (92 ¹/8 × 52)
The Art Institute of Chicago,
the Joseph Winterbotham
Collection

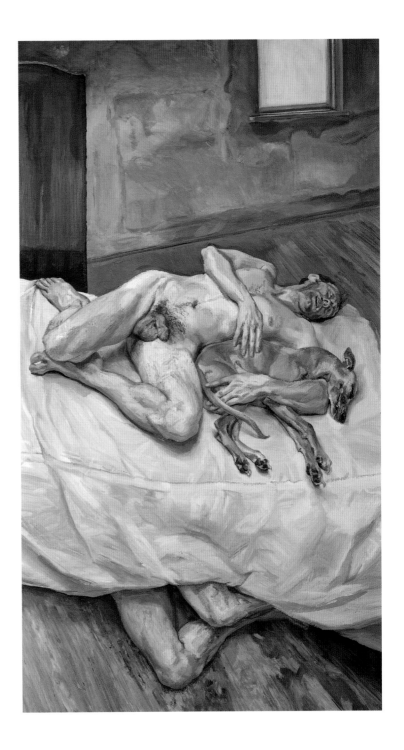

The Annunciation – which, in the hands of twentieth-century Realists, such as Balthus and Edward Hopper, had recently been renewed.

Such images circulate around the beholding of spectacular disclosures of the body. But sight, in some of Freud's paintings, remains, like the convex-mirrored self-portrait of Parmigianino, a compulsive gaze locked into a circuit of mesmeric self-reflection. This is the case for a large proportion of his self-portrayals and his reflection paintings, and it had been foreseen in his drawing *Narcissus* of 1950 (fig.4). The British Neo-Romantic convention of the narcissistic 'dreamy boy'[9] would be complicated and overthrown by Freud through a painterly and excessive augmentation of the existential doubt latent in the figure of Narcissus. But, to refocus on Freud's art in the 1940s, the iconography of narcissism remains important. Wallace Fowlie's essay for the 'Narcissus Issue' of *View* magazine in October 1943 makes compelling reading when laid alongside Freud's paintings and drawings from the 1940s and early 1950s. Fowlie placed the reflections on Narcissus of Freud's grandfather into the frame of contemporary art. Given Freud's familiarity with his grandfather's works and, more importantly, his personification of the young Romantic ego,[10] the significance of Narcissus, that doubting and desiring exemplary Modernist – according to Fowlie – as a phantasm of vision's self-sufficiency and the suspension of temporality, becomes compelling as a key element in assembling some of the early structures of his art.

Of Freud's *Narcissus* Stephen Bann has written: 'It is uneasy, as though the energy of self-scrutiny were displaced, and seeking for a home.'[11] Bann then discusses Freud's *Unfinished Self-Portrait* 1952 in terms of the problem of mirroring as representation: 'How is representation to break out of the circle of self-reflection? How is a refusal to admit the specular image to be translated into an engagement with other bodies and a painted surface no longer fractured but whole?'[12] Through recourse to a more tactile and painterly mode of working, in the late 1950s Freud broke and exceeded that narcissistic paradigm and has spent much of his time – up till the present – according closely observed bodies a form of alterity. Preceding this moment – which Robert Hughes places as being in 1958/9 with *Woman Smiling*[13] – is the melancholy crisis painting *Hotel Bedroom* 1954 (fig.5), with its conflicted gazes. Here, a surveilling stare of pent-up

4
Narcissus 1950
Pen and ink on paper
22.3 × 14.5 (9 1/8 × 5 3/4)
Private Collection

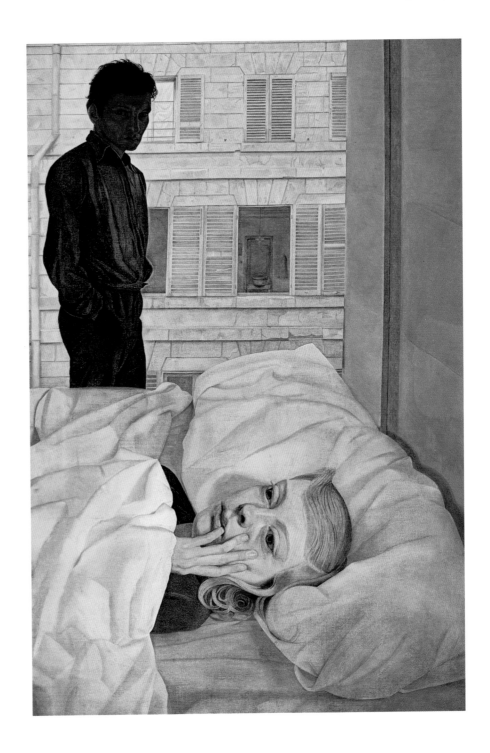

5
Hotel Bedroom 1954
Oil on canvas
91.1 × 61 (35 7/8 × 24)
The Beaverbrook Foundation,
The Beaverbrook Art Gallery,
Fredericton, NB Canada

6
**Reflection with Two Children
(Self-Portrait)** 1965
Oil on canvas
91.5 × 91.5 (36 ¹/₂ × 36 ¹/₂)
Museo Thyssen-Bornemisza,
Madrid

and dandified male mastery is directed to the painting's spectator, over
against a wounded female pathos.

This was over-looking in a mirrored world, a world of fraught intimacies,
where bodies become disjunctive. Later, Freud's *Small Interior (Self-Portrait)*
1968 used a Whistlerian or Sickertian over-mantel mirror play, but only to
diminish the scene, like the oxymoron of juxtaposed optical inflation and
diminution that was present in his *Reflection with Two Children (Self-Portrait)*
1965 (fig.6). Here, a complex path of looks from parent to child across
periscopic mirrors and domestic space is traced. Perverse perspectival play
was a commonplace of British painting in the twentieth century; it was,
for example, something to which Mark Gertler had attended in his self-
portrait in a convex mirror, and it had ample Mannerist precedent. Freud's

little homunculus stick-figure version of himself in *Small Interior (Self-Portrait)* 1968, a ragged Rumplestiltskin, is a consequence of a distorting anamorphic space. This space is also found, contemporaneously, in his colleague Francis Bacon's paintings – for example in the cut mirrors reflecting corporeal separation and wounds in *Study of George Dyer in a Mirror* 1968. While some of Freud's paintings titled 'Reflection' have suggested a closeness to reverie and kinds of self-observing absorption, many speak visually of a suspension in traumatic arrestation, of frozen watchfulness.

Freud's *Reflection with Two Children* might also be thought of as a complex anamorphic response to the segmentation of public images across differently scaled registers – the clashing sphere of bodily intimacies and Pop representations that artists such as Michael Andrews or James Rosenquist were addressing and creating divided spaces for in the early 1960s. Such tilted and anamorphic images – like the slanting mirror in Freud's 1965 *Self-Portrait* – form a link with the next section of this study. Arguably, Freud's most important graphic works are his illustrations for William Sansom's 1948 novel of drastic bodily disorder – *The Equilibriad*. In it Sansom played with bodily instability through the treacherousness of one-point perspective and photographic vision, anticipating the looming figure of the anamorphised paternal Freud in *Reflection with Two Children*, where 'the body towered away to a thin giddying distance'.[14]

8
Interior with Plant, Reflection Listening 1967–8
Oil on canvas
121.8 × 121.8 (48 ^{1}/8 × 48 ^{1}/8)
Private Collection

Wild Bodies

It was his body that seemed somehow to have lost its equilibrium
(WILLIAM SANSOM, *The Equilibriad* 1948)

A constant theme in Freud's visual imagination has been the presence
of unstable, spasmic human bodies, which appear to the spectator to be
in a state of strangeness. This is evident in recent works such as the
St Theresa-like ecstasies of the *Benefits Supervisor Resting* 1994 (fig.9), but
goes back to the disarticulation of the physiognomy of *John Minton* 1952
(fig.10). It may have been significant that prior to Freud's movement in
the 1950s away from the register of the Neo-Romantic fantastic to a more
Realist code of representation he had encountered a model for resolving
the imaging of the world as simultaneously familiar and incredible. This
encounter came about through his illustrations for William Sansom's
novella, *The Equilibriad* (1948), with its open appropriation of the schemas
of Franz Kafka. In the course of this short narrative, a forty-year-old
London office worker, Paul, wakes to discover himself in a predicament
echoing the grotesque morphing of Gregor Samsa into an insect in Kafka's
Metamorphosis of 1916: 'he attempted to lie squarely on his back . . . it
occurred to him then that he had indeed become a barrel.'[1] Paul is represented in constant paroxysm, overtaken by the specific pathological
condition, myasthenia, which induces radical bodily instability. As with
the painting *A Man Who Suddenly Fell Over* 1952, by Freud's associate
Michael Andrews, which depicts the male body in an Existential crisis,
Paul is perpetually on the verge of toppling over. This world of bodies
created by Sansom and illustrated by Freud was also reminiscent of the
dissociated phenomenology of the body outlined as early as the First
World War by Wyndham Lewis, in, for example, the stories contained in
The Wild Body (1927) – at once comic and grotesque.

In the text and illustrations, Paul is represented lurchingly, anamor-
phically; he exists aslant and sees the world asquint (fig.11). Like the
struggling Vincent van Gogh represented in the large oils painted by

9
Benefits Supervisor Resting 1994
Oil on canvas
160 × 150 (63 × 59 1/8)
Private Collection

Francis Bacon for his Hanover Gallery exhibition in 1957, he is a figure drawn out of the Existentialist imagination: 'sliding like a slanting shadow down the grey street'.[2] While Sansom's prose recovers an older Modernist Expressionist vision of a diagonalised metropolitan world – as with the scenics of Lyonel Feininger, Ernst Kirchner and Robert Wiene's *Cabinet of Dr. Caligari* (1919) – Freud's illustrations adhere to more contemporary visual styles. Arguably, he transmuted the figurative art of some of the Existentialist-inflected Parisian artists of the 1940s like Francis Gruber and André Fougeron. And, besides Kafka, Sansom was also using the literary and philosophical formulations of those French Existential writers who were emphasising the chancy contingencies of life, the refractory bodies, collapses and extremities of danger.[3]

But since this is a Continental literature of crisis re-worked for the stage of a shabby post-Victorian London, Freud draws Paul like a stocky Fougeron proletarian (indeed there may be a subterranean link here, in terms of style, to formats of Social Realism), but estranged – holding himself awkwardly, disequilibriated and barely hanging on to a rail in his office, where Kafka-esque shame, guilt and disaster lurk everywhere. Yet this aura of banality and catastrophe ultimately acts as a stimulus, a source of jubilation in the face of dread: 'a feeling of exaltation . . . this little attack . . . has put life into things. The very street is precarious! . . . He stood by the banister, swaying in an excess of excitement.'[4] This mix of elation and dread is compounded by Freud's drawing of Paul – recognisably in the guise of Freud himself – narrowly missing a collision with a street lamp but engrossed and fascinated by its presence (fig.31): '[He] noticed with misgiving and delight its hard iron corners, its black sharpness. A near one!'[5] The other three illustrations all dwell on a topic upon that Freud would endlessly elaborate in his art – that of gazing at, or falling under the gaze of others, of eyes wide open in scrutiny, like those of the caretaker's son who 'watched [Paul] closely' (fig.11, bottom left).[6]

Emerging from a complex cultural setting, Freud's exceptionality was partly shaped by his Central European marginality, as well as an adopted English Dandyism and anarchic bohemianism. Perhaps acknowledging the former, for his *Portrait of Lucian Freud* 1951, Bacon lent him the look and gaze of Kafka, copied from a photograph of the writer with his sister

10
John Minton 1952
Oil on canvas
40 × 25.4 (15 3/4 × 10)
Royal College of Art Collection

11
Four drawings from William
Sansom's **The Equilibriad** 1948

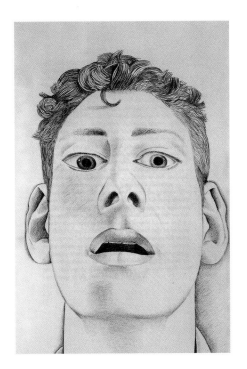 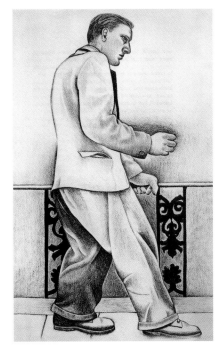

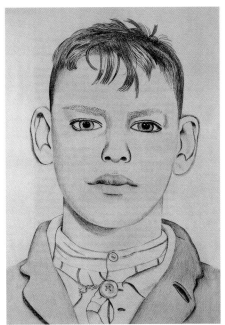 

Ottla from 1915.[7] The illustrations for *The Equilibriad* incorporate the Kafka-esque sensibility that was the key to much vanguard writing in London in the 1940s: Freud had, in fact, been familiar with Kafka's fictions from an early age. One of the additional conduits for Kafka's writing was Peter Watson's magazine *Horizon*, which was founded in 1939 and in whose orbit Freud first moved, along with Stephen Spender and Cyril Connolly. In 1943, Watson eulogised Kafka in a letter to John Craxton, who lived in an adjoining studio to Freud in St John's Wood in London. Watson wrote: 'Kafka symbolises and allegorises frustration which is the keynote of the present epoch, when every single belief and accepted custom is going to be challenged. No wonder artists have retreated into themselves so much in the last years. They are not likely to stop in my opinion.'[8] This identification of Kafka with the conflicted bodily and mental condition that Sigmund Freud termed *fehlleistung*, or parapraxis, in 1909,[9] casts a further light on the rich cultural matrix around Lucian Freud in his formative years. (It might, for instance, be possible to speculate on the harsh parapraxtic meanings present in the 1954 work *Hotel Bedroom* (fig.5).)

Freud not only engaged with the history of Modernism – with Paul Klee, Pablo Picasso, Giorgio de Chirico and Franz Kafka – but with the history of pre-Modernist artists such as Albrecht Altdorfer and Matthias Grünewald, as well as with that great shift, 'The Call to Order',[10] of the late 1910s and 1920s. The transgressive art of the Surrealists was also on the agenda of *Horizon*. Georges Bataille's thought and writing, which augmented that of Salvador Dalí, erupts in Freud's wartime drawings and paintings of dead animals. Richard Calvocoressi has discussed Freud's modalities of animal imagery around 1944 – his interest in horror and hybridity: 'The title page [of Nicholas Moore's *The Glass Tower* (1944)], designed by Freud, shows a sinister bird, half bird, half human, staring from a window . . . not unlike a mediaeval bestiary.'[11] Certainly, the presence of decomposing animals – substitutes for a lack of human models – disturbed Sir Kenneth Clark. However, the spectacle of animals preying on others or being devoured or in death was surfacing more generally in Neo-Romantic culture at this time.[12] These metaphors around existence and death in wartime cancelled the pathetic fallacy of the animal as a mirror of the human, stressing instead, a raw otherness of the creatural. As examples we might note Bacon's fascination with Eric Hosking's savage bird photographs, including that of the body of a fulmar with its 'dying struggles' imprinted in the sand, anticipating the position of Freud's *Dead Heron* 1945 (fig.12) of the following year.[13] Animal and human bodies in Freud's universe are inscribed with mortality, subdued and fundamentally unstable, each bearing the anti-Romantic, Naturalistic marks of a post-Darwinian world of extinctions and vertiginous existence.

The projection and modelling of hysterical signs upon Freud's bodies re-makes their meanings. Thus his late nude (and dressed) figures appear in states of oblivion. Where does this iconography of bodily abandonment come from? From Viennese figuration we could think of the example of Oskar Kokoschka's *Bride of the Winds* 1914, or of Gustav Klimt's *Medicine* 1900–7 and *Philosophy* 1898–90, nude figures tumbling in space. More recently, in the early 1980s, Robert Longo provided an iconography of hysteria and alienation in his 'Men in the Cities' series. (Yet another citation might be uncovered from the Surrealist iconography of the dreamer.)

12
Dead Heron 1945
Oil on canvas
49 × 74 (19 ¹/4 × 29 ¹/8)
Private Collection

Different forms of re-proportioning also inflect Freud's depictions of the figure. The compression of the body and enlargement of the head in *Small Interior (Self-Portrait)* 1968 and *Reflection with Two Children (Self-Portrait)*, lends the adult body a child's ratios.[14] This diminution is superseded by Freud's self-monumentalising as a small giant composed of paint deposits in *Painter Working, Reflection* 1993 (fig.13). The gargantuan body reaches a kind of apogee with the paintings of Leigh Bowery from around 1990. This vertiginous triumphalism of the upright body – the male figure confidently standing, as in *Two Men in the Studio* 1987–9 (fig.14) – might be thought about in relation to Linda Nochlin's strictures about Freud and phallocentricity,[15] as well as his management of comparable female postures where reverie, dreaming and weightlessness are thematised in paintings such as *Standing by the Rags* 1988–9 (fig.15) and *Lying by the Rags* 1989–90 (fig.41). The world-turned-upside-down of the carnivalesque is also apparent as a part of the signification of those nudes – both male and female – dating from around 1990 and after, where the figure floats above the floor or slides or slants in another version of the performance of suspension that is usually mimed by the frozen gaze of the eyes in Freud's work.

These low, genitally focused, oblivion-bound and levitating figures of Freud's iconography from the late 1980s onwards could be thought of in conjunction with Mikhail Bakhtin's observations on the carnivalesque and identification of the 'three main acts in the life of the grotesque body: sexual intercourse, death throes . . . and the act of birth . . . the same body that rises again, incessantly moving from the lower to the upper level'.[16] Such actions might also be indicative of a transgressive movement to 'escape the human limits of the body'.[17] In her essay for Freud's Whitechapel Gallery catalogue of 1993, Catherine Lampert also remarked on these 'air-borne fantasies'.[18] And, in the form of Leigh Bowery, the implications of a fallen angel suggested by his grandiose yet transgressive body image hints at a flight to escape the primary mark of sexual difference and the dichotomies of gender. What Mary Russo has called 'the labour of the fleshy sign'[19] drives towards an extraordinary transcendentalism of the gross ascending to the condition of 'the aerial sublime'.[20]

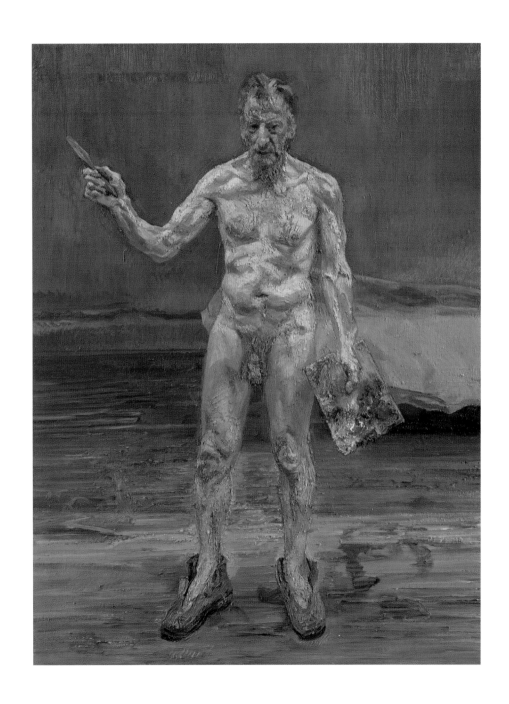

13
Painter Working, Reflection 1993
Oil on canvas
101.6 × 81.7 (40 × 32 ¹/₄)
Private Collection

14
Two Men in the Studio
1987–9
Oil on canvas
185.5 × 120.7 (73 × 47 ¹/₂)
Lewis Collection

(*opposite*) 15
Standing by the Rags
1988–9
Oil on canvas
168.9 × 138.4 (66 ¹/₂ × 54 ¹/₂)
Tate. Purchased with assistance
from the National Art Collections
Fund, the Friends of the Tate
Gallery and anonymous donors
1990

16
Francis Gruber **Woman on a Couch (Portrait of Madame Gruber)** 1945
Oil on canvas
130 × 161 (51 1/8 × 63 3/8)
Musée National d'Art Moderne, Paris

These gross material signs serve to recall us to Freud's unremitting specificities of place. In the third section of this book we shall consider the importance of built structures and the metropolitan shabbiness inhabited by these spectacular bodies. Freud's spare interiors continually suggest abjection; they recall a damper and coarser version of Francis Gruber's Parisian decors of the 1940s, where domestic frames expressed the same catastrophes of history and being that were allegorised in *The Equilibriad*. Gruber's melancholy – like that of Freud – is part of the more encompassing and international existential project of living on in the ruins of the West in a metaphorically and literal state of unsheltered-ness. This was a project to which *Horizon* magazine constantly returned, especially as the 1940s drew to a close. Where Freud may be especially compared with Gruber is in relation to the abandoned and mutised estrangement of the latter's female figures, such as *Woman on a Couch (Portrait of Madame Gruber)* 1945 (fig.16).[21]

Brutalist Zones

Barbary was going back to . . . the waste margins of civilisation that she knew, where other outcasts lurked and where questions were not asked.

(ROSE MACAULEY, *The World My Wilderness*, 1950)

Freud's Dandyism – encompassing, like no other British twentieth-century artist apart from Sickert and Bacon, so many different points across the subcultural social and sexual horizons of the last sixty years – needs location in the ragged cultural history of this time to be fully comprehensible. Quitting his shabby-gentile studio in St John's Wood, Freud moved to Delamere Terrace in Paddington, a wartime zone of dereliction, in 1943. He was inhabiting the ruins of London alongside those other survivors of the collapse of the developed Imperial centre – the semi-criminal inner-city marginals, the deserters, the migrants – the *felaheen* of a metropolitan West whom Oswald Spengler had prophesised in *The Decline of the West*.[1] Catherine Lampert has written of this elective milieu of 'people who existed outside regular employment – costermongers, villains and thieves – men who guarded their women and showed drunken, dangerous strength in the weekend street fights'. But, she states, 'Although Freud was stimulated by their company', he avoided the depiction of this environment as a metropolitan idyll in his work.[2] The 'villains and thieves' place Freud within a particular social climate and context specific to wartime and post-war austerity in London. Jacob Epstein, his first father-in-law, pejoratively characterised him as a wide boy denizen of this world when he furiously wrote of 'the spiv Lucian Freud'.[3] The Spiv was a flamboyant figure in the contemporary imagination – a dandy who lived by his wits, beyond the consensual codes of law-abiding National Austerity. In other words, from a certain point of view, Freud and his elected social environment were at one; or rather his bohemian camouflage was the masquerade of the Spiv.

There is a reminder here of an earlier moment in twentieth-century British art – and another moment of social masquerade – the Slade School's 'Coster Gang' of the immediately pre-Great War days. This exemplified a drive by an earlier visual arts vanguard to reinvigorate itself through the appropriation of 'low' metropolitan subcultures. Lisa Tickner, for example, has noted how C.R.W. Nevinson and other young artists adopted, around 1912, 'black jerseys, scarlet mufflers and caps and hats' in an imitation of Parisian *apaches*, considering themselves 'the terror of Soho'.[4] Then as now, the socio-geographic dynamics of contrasting localities became a crucial aspect of the art that was being produced in London. The American writer Lincoln Kirstein had met Freud and sat for a portrait in 1950. According to Kirstein, this was in a rude, divided London composed around the mythical poles of Limehouse and the West End, where 'public encounters became stormy . . . Bar-hopping with Lucian and his chums, Francis Bacon and Eduardo Paolozzi, ended up one night at the Pride of Whitby . . . Our sittings ended violently with fisticuffs in the crush bar of Covent Garden.'[5] These juxtapositions of high and low cultures and behaviour are indicative not only of the bohemianism of Bacon and Freud's circle, but also of a wider cultural iconography of a shared ground of brutality and elite or noble referents. An instance of this was a mytho-logical drawing by Freud, from the same moment and group as the *Narcissus*, which was described by Kirstein as depicting 'a Borstal Boy as Hercules'.[6] Freud was moving towards this kind of brutalist confrontation of asymmetric and raw signifiers, away from the arch and fantastic realm of Neo-Romance and Neo-Surrealism that he had been adept at building in paintings like *The Painter's Room* 1943–4 (fig.17). With its hunting-trophy zebra's head entering a diminished room, this work recapitulated the tactics of de Chirico and Max Ernst, but more exactly the travestying of Edwardian trophies that interested artists like Dalí. The latter begged a stuffed bear from his patron Edward James at his country seat, West Dean, in the mid-1930s in a kind of comic fetishising of Imperial trophies within a collapsed post-Imperial culture, a gesture that would be enacted thirty years later in the abject and melancholy contents of Steptoe and Son's yard.

The dramatic (and also comic) possibilities to be found in this unsheltered landscape of the West's ruination (which had preoccupied Francis Gruber) also informed the decor for the theatre of Samuel Beckett. (Peter Brooks had, unsuccessfully, tried to engage Bacon as a designer for his productions in the mid-1950s.) The accelerated spectacle of public squalor and privatised

17
The Painter's Room 1943–4
Oil on canvas
63.1 × 76.1 (24 3/4 × 29 7/8)
Private Collection

experience in the 1980s gave a new sumptuousness to this desolation. Freud's masterpiece *Large Interior W11 (after Watteau)* 1981–3 (fig.19), with its emphasis on the reverie of the young amidst a scene of desolation, was animated by the mix of voluminous and expensive fabrics along with the abject, stripped-plaster interior wall prior to renovation. This suggested an entire world of early 1980s culture and fashion in London: the dawning of the Thatcherite reduction of the public sphere, which contracted into a new primacy for reveries on the interior. The interiors of the Neo-Georgians at this time – their refusal of modernising good taste and their adoption of *brut* surfaces [7] – would find an echo, more than a decade and a half later, in Brian Kennedy's report of Freud's remarks:

18
Wasteground with Houses,
Paddington 1970–2
Oil on canvas
167 × 101 (65 3/4 × 39 3/4)
Private Collection

(*opposite*) 19
Large Interior W11 (after
Watteau) 1981–3
Oil on canvas
186 × 198 (73 1/4 × 78)
Private Collection

Freud says he likes things to be unembellished . . . He told me that when he moved into his old house in London, he had lots of wallpaper removed, and when he finally got to the surface and found it yellow and marked with a line made by the rising damp, he liked the way that it looked and decided to leave it that way. This is the damp line on the wall that appears as a sort of horizon line, a marvellous yellow and green landscape in *After Cézanne* 2000 (fig.25).[8]

Freud avoided the conventionalised clichés of sentimental genre, and instead helped create, and then extend, forms of Modernist Realism that conserved and eroticised estrangement in the world of perceived post-war decline. Similarly, Rose Macauley, in her novel *The World My Wilderness* (1950) traced the new spaces of metropolitan desolation populated by adolescent bohemian bodies, like those in Freud's *Large Interior W11*. When Macauley wrote this short novel at the end of the 1940s, she was being published in *Horizon*, and was a friend of Freud's patron, Stephen Spender. Her narrative, set in 1946, centred upon Barbary, a young Anglo-French painter at The Slade. She and her colleague, a boy called Raoul, are waif-like refugees from the Maquis at Collioure, and are thus marked by that key word from the foundation of Modernism: *fauves* (wild animals). This is emphasised by Barbary's name and description as 'a watchful little animal or savage'.[9] She and Raoul, like Winston Smith and Julia on their ruined metropolitan idyll in George Orwell's *1984* (1950), move across a bombed London stage recalling that of T. S. Eliot's *The Wasteland* (1922). From his vantage point in North Kensington, Freud has painted these wasteland spaces, such as *Wasteground with Houses, Paddington* 1970–2 (fig.18), with its tangles of nameless rubbish items lying at the bottom of the painting in skeins of abjection, hemmed in by wood fencing and brick wall. In works like *Large Interior W11*, he has also presented the marginal space of the apparently set-aside past, a hermetic space for day-dreaming and wasted bodies.

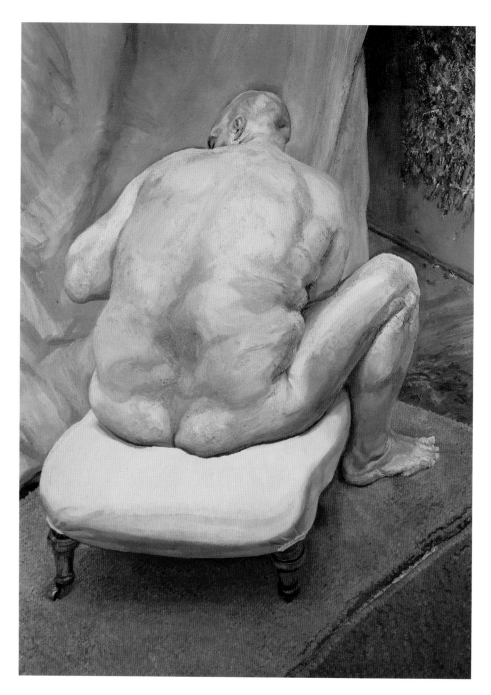

20

Naked Man, Back View 1991–2
Oil on canvas
182.9 × 137.2 (72 × 54)
The Metropolitan Museum of Art,
Purchase, Lila Acheson Wallace
Gift, 1993 (1993.71)

Masquerades

Like me, he is interested in the underbelly of things

(LEIGH BOWERY, *c.*1993)

21
Torso Belvedere (first century BC)
Marble
Vatican Museums and Galleries,
Vatican City, Rome

With his paintings of Leigh Bowery's gargantuan bodily frame, Freud extended – perhaps even more fully than Bacon did – a de-idealised tradition of the grotesque nude. One place to begin to chart Freud's depiction of heroic bodily excess might be *Naked Man, Back View* 1991–2 (fig.20): massive, crouched and with the bulky head averted and disappearing. Ingres *The Valpinçon Bather* 1808 has been cited as a comparative painting,but other possible imagings of the body from behind could be considered, ones that also fray the lines between bulk and sexuality. The great prototype of such a figure is the *Torso Belvedere* (first century BC) (fig.21) in the Vatican's Museo Pio-Clementina, which occupies a crucial place in the representation of the body in the West. That it was read as an object of sublime excess by Johannes Wincklemann, who identified it as an image of Hercules,[1] is not entirely at odds with an alternative identification of the statue as the hero of the Trojan wars, Philoctetes, whose snakebite festered and smelled abominably, causing him to be marooned in Lemnos – mighty but stigmatised and abject, like Bowery. For Bowery was lodged in the register of the colossal, described by Freud as a figure with 'Gigantic modesty and an enormous presence'.[2] This corporeal bulk introduces a reminder of the art of Pavel Tchelitchew, specifically that of 1935–8, in his studies around his large oil, *Phenomena*, which consisted of bulging heterotopic bodies and anamorphic projections, and which Freud could have encountered in Peter Watson's collection.[3]

Yet it might be said that Bacon's versions of the male body are the prime ghosts haunting the Bowery series. There is some recollection, in that back view of the Australian Leigh Bowery, of a painting by Bacon that has been in Melbourne at the National Gallery of Victoria since 1953 – *Study from the Human Body* 1949. Freud would have seen it in 1949 or

1950, when it was on show at the Hanover Gallery, London, at the moment when he began his friendship with Bacon. Perhaps this back view becomes some kind of superhuman painted phantasm of homosexual experience – the existential mode of 'courage' that Freud told Bowery he admired.[4] The low pouffe on which Bowery is sitting presents the same kind of round-ended contour, projecting out of the picture, that functioned for Bacon as a platform device for the display of troubled and sexualised bodies, and which he had used in paintings such as the 'hypodermic' mattress portraits of 1963 and 1964, and for *Henrietta Moraes* 1966. Another determinant of the Bowery series may have been the Bacon painting that Freud owned: *Two Figures* 1953, with its poised, weighted, emphatically queer and exulting bodies. Like *Study from the Human Body*, in *Two Figures* there are grey curtains and a kind of rifted zone at the back of the picture. So Freud, in the year of Bacon's death, appeared to be in a sort of dialogue with his art and the tensions of the male body and its desires.

From the 1940s onward, Freud had been forging a kind of uncanny picture-making – in his grandfather's terms, an *unheimliche* or unhomely world of disturbed shelter. This could be called a pictorial staging ground for human patterns of narcissism and hysteria, for the distracted, staring sitters and collapsing, Kafka-esque metropolitans, who even when they were at home (such as in Freud's own ambiguous domestic territory in *Large Interior W11*), were drastically displaced. Marginals and the estranged, we have seen, hold a special place on this uncanny but Realist stage – the procurer, for example, with his gangland contacts (fig.22), or the desperate little man.[5] Bowery – a gay performance artist and costume designer – holds his place in this file chiefly on account of his extraordinary corporeality. What Allon White has referred to as 'the site of grotesque realism'[6] could almost be the epigraph for an analysis of Freud's style.

It was, perhaps, Bowery's protean abilities to erase boundary markers of gender and transform himself into an unclassifiable hybrid made up of flesh and dress that drew Freud to him:

Because I'm chubby, I can pleat the flesh across my chest and hold it in place with heavy grade gaffer tape. Then, by wearing a specially

22
The Procurer (Man in a Headscarf) 1954
Oil on canvas
32.5 × 22.3 (12 3/4 × 8 3/4)
Private Collection

constructed underpadded, up-lift bra, I create the impression of a heaving bosom with a six inch cleavage. Rather than dance with my penis flopping about, I do a tuck and glue job to affect a hairy pussy.[7]

However, by emphasising Bowery's penis in his naked paintings of him, Freud shifted the artifice of this constructed, performed, self-fashioned hybridity.

In early October 1988, Bowery placed himself under the sign of narcissistic self-absorption and display by posing at the Anthony d'Offay Gallery on a *chaise-longue* in front of a one-way mirror, seeing himself – differently costumed each day for a week – but also being observed by his audience.[8] Freud might have found reflected in the conditions, form and content of this tableau some of his own concerns that have been traced in this book: the gaze of Narcissus and the spectacle of de-idealised flesh. The grotesque, we could say, was crucial to the Bowery/Freud partnership: 'Like me', Bowery told the *Australian Herald*, ' [Freud] is interested in the underbelly of things'.[9]

Any conceptualisation of the category of the grotesque, will, following the writings of the Russian critic Mikhail Bakhtin on Rabelais, lead towards the zone of the belly and the dynamics of a social underbelly. What Bahktin, in the 1940s, called the 'materialism of the belly',[10] is present in a literal and allegoric form in Freud's pictorial translations of the bodies of Leigh Bowery and Sue Tilley, the equally massive Benefits Officer (fig.9). Other commentators have remarked on the priority accorded by Freud to the forehead and frontal lobe, but there is a similar and just as telling significance to the globular belly in *Leigh Under the Skylight* 1994. In this work, Freud plaits together the twin strands of the base materialism of flesh and of complex masquerade. The figure of the colossus is also that of the triumphant Fool, raised high, surrounded by Freud's bare scenography of stained walls and skylight. Here is the carnivalesque Fool as a true Gargantua, reigning over the motley crowd of English bizarre that Freud had assembled during the 1980s, and which had included the etiolated Watteau-esque crowd in *Large Interior W11* and the paintings of the Supplementary Benefits Officer. While they are brute Realist in style and execution, the route for these works can be traced back

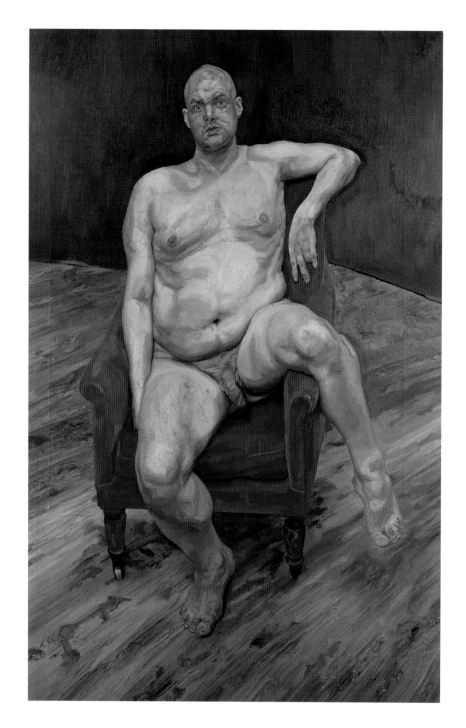

23
Leigh Bowery (Seated) 1990
Oil on canvas
243.8 × 182.9 (96 × 72)
Mr and Mrs Richard C. Hedreen

24
Nude with Leg Up 1992
Oil on canvas
183 × 228.5 (72 × 90)
Hirshhorn Museum and Sculpture Garden,
Smithsonian Institution. Joseph H. Hirshhorn
Purchase Fund 1993

to that guiding moment for the French and English Neo-Romantics at the beginning of the twentieth century – Picasso's Rose period. Seen in this way, the towering Bowery becomes a variant of the buffoon in the large saltimbanque family canvas of Picasso, or Apollinaire as Picasso envisaged him, as a huge athlete with enormous musculature in the drawing *La Culture Physique* 1907.[11] George T. Noszopoly has suggested that Picasso's representations of Apollinaire in this carnivalesque mode are 'bordering on the mock-heroic'.[12] It is this ambivalence between the grotesque and the colossal, between ennoblement and the abject, that marks these paintings by Freud, but which also leads back into the ambivalences not only of the social carnival, but also of Neo-Romanticism itself.

But there was a more immediate context for Freud's paintings of Bowery: that of contemporary Performance art. Indeed, frameworks for the understanding of Freud had shifted in the course of the 1980s. By the end of the decade there had been an avalanche of claims that sought to place Freud in terms of a certain Realism associated with the category of The School of London, a curatorial invention of R. B. Kitaj from the second half of the 1970s. But it may be more significant to locate Freud instead in the climate of the postmodern attention to the body and to the new prominence given to the performing self. Essentially, Freud re-emerged against the field of corporeal visual politics in the late 1980s and 1990s. It was, therefore, no coincidence that he joined forces with Bowery at a time of growing visibility for Performance and Body art in London. In 1988, the landmark Clerkenwell 'Edge 88' festival of performance culminated in the spectacle of Leigh Bowery's week of chaise-longue performances at Anthony d'Offay,[13] when metropolitan subcultural club styles crossed over into the context of an international avant-garde gallery.[14]

'In Britain, the lack of a masked carnival tradition is to some extent compensated for by the gay and fetish club scene', Roger Malbert has written:

> where people recreate themselves and parade as outlandishly as any Regency 'monstrosity'. The most famous exponent of transgressive masquerade in London in the 1980s and early 90s was Leigh Bowery, performance artist and costume designer . . . his carnivalesque disguises

and distortions of his gargantuan frame are legendary . . . [a] performance with Nicola Bowery re-enacts a traditional carnival masquerade – the fat man giving birth – which occurs in the *commedia dell'arte*.[15]

In Freud's paintings Bowery appears as a vast androgyne whose belly suggests such a pregnancy, anticipating the vast belly of Sue Tilley. Flesh has become more than an excess; it contains a parody of pregnancy in the swelling of paint as body mass. If, as Nicholas Penny reports,[16] Freud was influenced by Aubrey Beardsley *c.*1940, then the buffoonery of grotesque Symbolism, in its incorporation of *commedia dell'arte* roles, might also have been smuggled into his sensibility. If this is the case, Freud has maintained a cynical and sardonic identification with this iconographic range, apparently rejecting its idyllic and pastoral aspects. Yet the theatricalisation of pictorial terms may be vital to understanding Freud's *mise en scène*. It is perhaps present in his recent painting, *After Cézanne* 2000 (fig.25), which stages the revenant appearance of Cézanne's grotesque carnival of bodies, *Afternoon in Naples* 1866–7. Here, Freud has read the Cézanne as 'a farce'; it is as if the Cézanne were the travesty while Freud's is the rectified version. Perhaps this extraordinarily ambitious painting corresponds to the revisionary ratio that Harold Bloom sketched in his study *Anxiety of Influence* as the *Apophrades*, or the return of the dead. In Bloom's scheme, the advent of the *Apophrades* marks the point at which 'the later poet, in his final phase, already burdened by an imaginative solitude that is almost a solipsism, holds his own poem open again to the precursor's work'.[17] Bloom refers to the 'uncanny effect' of the precursor artist scripting the work. Thus, we could speculate that Freud, in his lofty late period, looks back to Cézanne, fully acknowledging the condition of being 'after' the great precursor of Modernism and rendering this belatedness as a moment of estranged bedroom farce.

The realisation of a theatricalised comic tableau can be strongly sensed in Bruce Bernard's photographs taken in Freud's studio during 1991–5 (fig.27). In these, performance is playfully replayed – Nicola Bowery doubling her pose in the painting, the colossus of Leigh Bowery under the skylight, standing to the right of the oil of him. But most of all, this theatrical repetition is present in a photograph that became a kind of

25
After Cézanne 2000
Oil on canvas
214 × 215 (84 1/4 × 84 5/8)
Collection: National Gallery of
Australia, Canberra. Purchased with
assistance of members of the NGA
Foundation, including David Coe,
John Schaeffer and Kerry Stokes AO,
2001

26
William Rothenstein
The Doll's House 1899–1900
Oil on canvas
88.9 × 61 (35 × 24)
Tate. Presented by
C.L. Rutherston, 1917

performance piece in itself, illustrating Bowery's interview with Freud
'Art and Love', in *The Independent Magazine* in January 1992. Here
Courbet's *The Artist's Studio* 1855 is parodied, with the muse shifting sex
to the ambiguously bodied Bowery, and with Freud and Bowery taking up
the positions of the artist and model in Courbet's picture. In fact, *After
Cézanne* recalls those Symbolist theatrical allegories that were crucial
to early twentieth-century British artists, such as William Rothenstein
and Augustus John, in pictures like Rothenstein's *The Doll's House*
1899–1900 (fig.26), which cited Ibsen. The difference between those
turn-of-the-century dramas and Freud's turn-of-the-new-century scenarios
is the imaging of a male rather than a female crisis.

The larger dramatisation of social dissonance by Freud can be found
across his career, going back to his earliest paintings and drawings of the

27
Lucian Freud and Leigh Bowery
imitate the poses of the artist and
model in Courbet's *The Artist's
Studio* of 1855
Photograph by Bruce Bernard,
1992

1940s. It can be found in the grotesque physiognomies of the *faux-naif* drawings made *c*.1940, for instance, in the *fumiste* caricatural heads of Stephen Spender and Cyril Connolly of 1940, which can be compared with the vast-headed profiles of George Grosz.[18] In terms of the development of Realism in the modernist period, Grosz might be regarded as an important precursor to Freud. His reception in England during the 1920s and 1930s depended on the one hand on the initiatives of Edward Burra, who parasitised him in his satires of sexual subcultures, and on the other, on the Leftist graphic caricaturists around *Left Review* in the mid-1930s. Certainly, by the late 1930s Grosz was clearly seen less as an exotic in English visual culture than as a prime figure in the mediation of the concept of German style and sensibility that the cultural historian Peter Sloterdijk has dubbed 'Cynical Realism'. Sloterdijk located this within the nihilist currents in Weimar thought and culture, enshrining Grosz as a key figure and enunciator of this mentality.[19] In 'The artist's preface' to *Uber alles die Liebe* (1930), Grosz admitted the true temper of this Cynical Realism of absolute transparency and objectivity: 'The title shows that the subject here is interpersonal relations . . . but don't expect my drawings to illustrate any run of the mill lover's idyll. Realist that I am, I use my pen and brush primarily for taking down what I see and observe, and what is generally unromantic, sober and not very dreamy . . . Sober and with no mystery!'[20] If we begin to imagine some frames of reference for Freud's works, particularly those of the last fifty years, Grosz's prioritisation of astringent observation might be one point of departure. As Rolf Lauter has recently shown, from his childhood Freud had enjoyed some degree of familiarity with Grosz's drawings: 'Grosz's works were also not unknown in the Freud house, at least in the form of publications.'[21] His *Ecce Homo* portfolio was in the household, with one of the prints bearing a dedication to Freud's architect father.

Additionally, we could say that the grotesque otherness of Leigh Bowery re-introduced the old social carnival of monstrous physiognomies and bodies that Freud had encountered with Grosz. Freud has generated a comparable carnival of caricatures of nihilist metropolitan existence to those of Grosz – for example, the drawing of Francis Bacon, with his flies part undone, of 1951 (fig.28), or the absurd romantic pairing in *And the*

28
Francis Bacon 1951
Pencil and charcoal on paper
54.7 × 42 (21¹/2 × 16¹/2)
R.B. Kitaj

Bridegroom of 1993 (fig.29). Certainly Grosz and Freud share a strong cultural pessimism, a pessimism that is almost Eliotic in the case of *After Cézanne*. The world depicted is apparently lacking all consolation and is unadorned save for the skin of the body itself, which in the case of Bowery, for instance, or Sue Tilley, takes on a 'disenchanted profligacy',[22] a 'defiance through sarcasm or the grimace',[23] the laughter of a de-sacralised world escaping from banality.

29
And the Bridegroom 1993
Oil on canvas
231.8 × 196.2 (91 ¹/4 × 77 ¹/4)
Lewis Collection

30
Girl with a White Dog 1950–1
Oil on canvas
76.2 × 101.6 (30 × 40)
Tate. Purchased 1952

Seeing a Body of Paint

A face approached, a contact with a skin – a face weighed down with a skin
(EMMANUEL LEVINAS)

31
Drawing from William Sampson's
The Equilibriad 1948

In his illustration 'Street Scene' for William Sansom's novel, *The Equilibriad* (fig.31), Freud dramatically describes the enchantment of the eye caught up in the flesh of the world.[1] Disturbingly, he incorporates into the bottom-left corner his own truncated self portrait, staring wide-eyed at the spectator. The bricks on the street wall in this drawing are minutely itemised in relief, in their pitted state, while the spectator's gaze crosses the challenge of the artist's own apotropaic eyes, passing beyond the bricks, in this intimate and proximate space, up and over the wall coping and back to the openings in the Victorian villa or terrace behind. The lamp standard's top, like Van Eyck's convex mirror in *The Arnolfini Marriage* 1434, performs the role of displaying the surfaces and metaphors of visibility – a source of light, with curved glass, harbouring reflections, like the eyes or glasses of Freud's sitters. As with the domestic ceiling lights in *Reflection with Two Children* 1965 (fig.6), the lamp gives some token of Freud's engrossment in nocturnal vision.

Since the early 1950s Freud has passed – formally speaking – from a flat linearity to more weighty volumes of paint and volume. But his romance of and with the eye has been central and constant; it was a crucial motif for the first part of his career and remains so today. First it was expressed in gleaming, excessive, over-large eyes, hyper-real, glassed, mirrored or naked – like those in 'Street Scene'. Freud has always located the optic in terms of flesh. Between 1945 and 1957, he gave a particular graphic designation to the liminal flesh of the lower eyelid – that lubricated internal rim, a curving frame and boundary between sight and flesh, a sickle sight.

While such a figuring might be thought to offer a straight route to Surrealist iconographies of the eye,[2] it also cleaves to a fascination with Flemish and German traditions of optical clarity that were reborn with figurative artists in Europe and North America in the 1920s. Perhaps the most formative moment for this kind of Modernist figuration was the exhibition *Neue Sachlichkeit*, held at the Kunsthalle, Mannheim in 1925. This tendency was given a number of descriptive titles. According to the the Kunsthalle's director Gustav Hartlaub, it was a 'New Objectivity' whose practitioners 'have retained or regained their fidelity to positive tangible reality'. The critic Franz Roh, however, in his book of the same year, *Nach Expressionismus – Magischer Realismus/Probleme der neuesten Europaischen Malerei*, held this new naturalism to be a 'Magical Realism' rather than objectivity. Roh prioritised the enchantment of the eye and the spectacle of the world, identifying participants across an international range from Pablo Picasso and André Derain to the younger German artists.[3] It is possible to consider Freud in relation to this invented twentieth-century tradition: for example, *Interior in Paddington* 1951 (fig.33) – like his illustrations for *The Equilibriad* – might be imagined in some sort of relation to the bizarre particularities of the marginal urban worlds of Karl Hubbuch. Or, if we plunge into the depths of Freud's painting, the loitering youth across the road, framed in the balcony railings, can be compared with Otto Dix's *Der Streicholzhandler II* 1927 (fig.32) as a delinquent street boy, one more of the 'lurkers on the margin'.[4] He can also be seen as an urban, pastoralised peasant, a modernised loiterer from Bruegel, or, as a foetally large-headed adolescent, an asphalt Philipp Otto Runge. With Freud, as with Dix, the overwhelming modernist iconography of childhood – part *faux-naif* Neo-Romantic, descending ultimately from Runge, and part disabused by Sigmund Freud's revelations of infantile sexuality – is mobilised and finds compellingly powerful new forms.

In Freud's work, a particular model of art and history drawn from the imperatives of an eternal Magical Realism, which the inter-war period had promoted, operates strongly. Like Dix, like Balthus and like Bacon, Freud refused that version of modernity that gave weight to processes of change, innovation and novelty. Similarly, in 1927 Dix wrote: 'In recent years, one catchphrase has motivated the current generation of creative artists. It urges them to "find new forms of expression". I very much doubt, however, whether such a thing is possible. Anyone who looks at the paintings of the Old Masters . . . will surely agree with me.'[5] Freud turned instead to

32
Otto Dix
Der Streicholzhandler II 1927
Oil on canvas
120 × 65 (47 1/4 × 25 1/2)
Stadtische Kunsthalle Mannheim

33
Interior in Paddington 1951
Oil on canvas
152.4 × 114.3 (60 × 45)
Walker Art Gallery,
National Museums and
Galleries on Merseyside

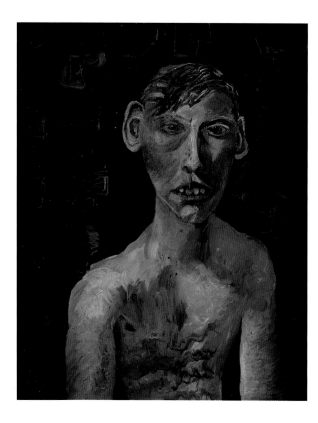

34
Evacuee Boy 1942
Oil on canvas
74.3 × 58.1 (29 1/4 × 22 7/8)
Private Collection

an arresting of time of the sort that the critic Georges Moulin had detected
in Balthus's work, outlined in an essay in *Cahiers d'Art* in 1946. Writing the
year before Freud and Balthus became close in Paris, Moulin explored the
metaphysics of romantic love as a countervailing force to modernism's
empirical and positivist accounts of love: 'The joy of love stops time,
which is the only eternity and with which man has never experimented.'[6]
Balthus's arrested construction of temporality and desire, of infancy
and adulthood, has clear similarities with Freud's projected world, the
childlike or *naif* air he gave his sitters through a slight enlargement of
the cranium, his approach to space and time. Sigmund Freud's term for
such an atemporality as a mode of experience was *zeitlos* – 'timeless'.

   The formation of a history of art that could timelessly preserve the past
alongside the drifts and desires of the present was also the aim of several
of the international brokers of the Magical Realist and Neo-Romantic style:

individuals such as Peter Watson, who wanted Freud and Craxton to look at his reproductions of both Picasso *and* Altdorfer in 1942.[7] The widely reported fact that Freud's grandfather gave him colour reproductions of the works of Bruegel the elder, suggests that, as well as being familiar with Dürer and Altdorfer, Freud had a grounding in sixteenth-century Northern art. Bruegel's social pastorals of essential peasant life, with their idlers and spectacles of vice, fit well with a narrative of London life such as *Interior at Paddington*. His graphic presence may also be found in the drawing *Loch Ness from Drumnadrochit* 1943 (fig.35). In relation to this, compare Bruegel's drawings of landscapes, particularly the panoramic and minutely mapped Alpine landscapes, after his journey to Italy, from the mid and late 1550s, such as *Mountain Landscape*, in The British Museum.[8]

It was into this matrix of history, where, as Lincoln Kirstein wrote in 1947, the 'speech of Western draughtsmanship' was 'set and almost

35
Loch Ness from Drumnadrochit
1943
Pen and ink on paper
37.2 × 45.4 (14 5/8 × 17 7/8)
Private Collection

ageless',[9] that Freud emerged in the late 1940s and early 1950s. We could imagine him co-existing in an alternative history of art, where, for example, the 1940s in New York would be concentrated around the predominance of Neo-Romantic and Magical Realist figuration, rather than the naissance of Abstract Expressionism. Kirstein is a key international figure here, prime mover of such consensus-generating exhibitions as MoMA's *American Realists and Magic Realists* in 1943. It was Kirstein who in 1950 brought to the recently inaugurated ICA in London a show of American Symbolic Realists, which Peter Watson welcomed. Their key stylistic characteristic was a hallucinatory optical precision, and this concentration on sharp focus indicates Freud's formal affiliations with American artists such as Ben Shahn, Louis Gugliemi, Jared French, Andrew Wyeth and Ivan Albright. There was some visibility for these American figurative artists in London in the late 1940s: for instance, Ben Shahn's painting was not only exhibited in May 1947, when fifteen of his paintings were shown at the Mayor Gallery, but Penguin also published a monograph in the 'Modern Painters' series by J.T. Soby in the same year. Yet Shahn's strong humanitarian Leftism might have repulsed the anti-idyllic Freud as much as attracting him with his inner-city street scenes and bright-eyed, nervously alert adolescents and children engaged in a kind of neurotic carnival (his *Liberation* of 1945, for example).

A major historical paradigm for this optically enhanced Magical Realism was the sixteenth-century painter, Hans Holbein. He had been singled out in Grosz's *Die Geizeichneten (The Marked Men)* 1930, where a caricatured *Neue Sachlichkeit* painter has a volume marked 'Holbein' under his easel. Holbein's *The Body of the Dead Christ in the Tomb* 1521–2 was the central referent in Dostoyevsky's *The Idiot* (1869), a novel that Freud knew well, having had it read aloud to him by his sitter, his second wife, Caroline Blackwood, in Paris in the early 1950s. Regarding Freud in the context of the existential imagination of the late 1940s and early 1950s suggests the salience of Dostoyevsky as a formulator of a vision of pitiless illumination where there is an intense scrutiny of the given, gross material world and a lack of cultural setting, of 'scenery',[10] with which Freud might have found an affinity.

The eye's surveillance in *The Idiot* summons up the panic world that Freud increasingly laid out in his paintings and drawings of the human body. As in the illustrations to *The Equilibriad*, the experience of being under another's gaze is a primary theme. Prince Myshkin increasingly falls under the searching eyes of others, primarily those of Rogozhin, whose 'eyes are fixed upon him',[11] haunting and pursuing him across St Petersburg in the melodramatic second part of the novel. And to be under suveillance in this way – the kind of surveillance necessary to his portraiture that Freud had written about in his 1953 *Horizon* statement – also necessitated an absolute illumination, such that 'a blinding *inner* light flooded his soul'.[12]

The implacable gaze that looks upon the existential bareness of things – such as the body of Christ in the novel – constitutes a basic structure in Freud's painting. In *The Idiot*, the gaze precipitates epilepsy, a stare that suggests the trace of a traumatic memory imprinted and relived, or the arrest of hysteria, the counterpart of the traumatised frozen watchfulness in Freud's work. In the novel, Prince Myshkin remarks of *Dead Christ*, 'Why, some people may lose their faith by looking at that picture.'[13] Like some of Freud's early paintings, it depicts a dead being in a truthful style, with a power to disillusion, to make atheists. This dolorous spectacle entails an emptying out of pathos and a recourse to ascetic strategies, enabling an uncanny verism, just as with Freud's work. Julia Kristeva has adopted *Dead Christ* as an example of melancholia. Its effect of closely observed isolation, she asserts, presents a metaphor of bodily presence 'without a beyond'.[14] In such a way, Holbein traces the empiricism of a world deserted by God, with no potential transcendence. In the harsh light of his readings of Nietzsche (and perhaps the Holocaust), Freud also views the world in this fashion.

Freud's aim to go beyond history (to reside with Rubens, Watteau and the ancient Egyptian artists of Armarna) stands outside time. In this sense, Emmanuel Levinas's idea of the human face standing apocalyptically outside history, time and space comes to mind.[15] For Freud, this revelatory face is most evident in the lyrical and visionary portraits of around 1948–52. Yet it is superseded by a shift from the gaze to the body, to the flesh as embodied sight, as Maurice Merleau-Ponty and Levinas were theorising in the 1950s. The mechanisms of otherness, of alterity, as Levinas described

36
Girl in a Dark Dress 1951
Oil on canvas
40.6 × 30.5 (16 × 12)
Private Collection

them in *Otherwise Than Being*, depend on proximity and the apparition of
the face. Just as Freud wishes to stand outside time, so Levinas considered
that the experience of the proximity of the other's face radically disturbed
temporality: 'Proximity is a disturbance of the rememberable time. One
could call that apocalyptically the break up of time . . . the present is but
a trace of an immemorial present.'[16] The marking of proximity had, after
all, been integral to Cézanne's art. The Cézannian experience of closely
regarded proximate surfaces, the intimacy of the objects beheld as points
of contact through reflected light, is reiterated in Freud's concentration on
the body's leading edges – the stomach, or, as Gowing noted, more often
the forehead: 'He has put more of the human forehead, for example, into
pictures than you could gather in the whole previous history of painting.'[17]
Gowing, as a scholar of Cézanne, must have been particularly sensitive to

this aspect of proximate surfaces in Freud's work; his comments point to a dynamic in Freud that takes its momentum from the new avidity he experienced in the mid and late 1950s to depict the lived volumes of the human body.

This drive towards bodily volume may have been prompted, it has been suggested, by the artist's observation of the connotations of depth in Bacon's paint.[18] It also has links to the existential Realism of Alberto Giacometti and to Cubism. With the three-part explorations of *Man's Head (Self-Portrait III)* 1963 (fig.38) there are echoes of Picasso's stereometry of Fernande's head, both painted and sculpted in bronze in 1909 (fig.37). Facial bulk would, of course, become more spectacularly thematised in his work of around 1990, but with the *Man's Head (Self-Portrait III)* there is a quasi-Cubist building of physiognomic planes of flesh as self-acknowledging paint, through the turning and multiplying of viewpoints, as well as through formal rhymes and repetitions. In 1992, Freud spoke to William Feaver of: 'forms repeated throughout the body and often in the head as well, so that you can see certain rhythms set up ... the insides and undersides of things ... something which would actually be visible from another position.'[19]

Such bodily invocations draw Freud closer into the net of a phenomenological criticism that has examined the modes by which Modernists, from Courbet, have achieved a sense of the lived body in space. For instance, from Michael Fried's Merleau-Ponty-inflected interpretations of Courbet have come analyses of lived space apprehended in the imagery of fleshy hands.[20] Comparably, in Freud's *Large Interior W11* (fig.19), there is an array of differently scaled hands, where touch – the playing of the mandolin; the hand on the boy's leg – plays a significant role in terms of familial tactility. There is a set of chromatic, metonymous linkages here – from paint to hands,[21] from hands to body – as can also be found in Bacon's work. Such a tracing of flesh as an indexical pictorial sign of volume is tantamount to a strategy of transubstantiation of the known and proximate body. As Freud said to Lawrence Gowing: 'I want paint to work as flesh ... I would wish my portraits to be of the people, not like them. Not having the look of the sitter, being them ... As far as I'm concerned the paint is the person.'[22] This transubstantiation of paint as flesh, the materials and pigment becoming skin, is a transaction to which Freud had

37
Pablo Picasso
Head of a Woman (Fernande) 1909
Plaster
40.5 × 23 × 26 (16 × 9 × 10 ¹/₄)
Tate. Lent from a private collection 1994

38
Man's Head (Self-Portrait III) 1963
Oil on canvas
30.5 × 25.1 (12 × 9 ⁷/₈)
National Portrait Gallery, London

alluded as early as his 1953 *Horizon* statement, where life became art: 'Painters who use life itself as their subject matter working with their object in front of them, or constantly in mind, do so in order to translate life into art almost literally, as it were.'[23] In his long essay 'Gedenken über Lucian Freud', Rolf Lauter has compared Freud's concentration on the face and his concern with the process of ageing with Oscar Wilde's *Picture of Dorian Grey* (1890): 'the painted picture of the person assumes the function of substituting for the real person.'[24]

The point, perhaps, is a bigger one revolving around the conceptualisation of the relationships of art and life in Symbolism and its Modernist destiny. Oscar Wilde famously put his art into his life – the Aestheticist presumption – while Freud, in the lineage of anti-Aestheticist Realists such as Sickert, puts the premium on the appropriation of lived existence. A possible connection between these two positions in the ancestry of British Modernism and between the figures of Wilde and Freud is the inscription of Aestheticism in the figure of the Dandy. Freud's Dandyism, like that of Walter Sickert, is intricate. Apparently downwardly mobile (in the early 1940s from St John's Wood to a bombed-out and derelict Paddington, close to the inverted pastoral of West London that Wyndham Lewis called 'Rotting Hill'), he also suffuses his self-portraits with a Regency coldness and elegance descending from Delacroix's *Baron Schwiter* 1826–30. With his portraits of the androgynous Leigh Bowery, Freud fulfilled the designated role of the Dandy, who challenges all founda- tional rules and divisions of the culture. Certainly, the *de haut en bas* gaze of *Reflection with Two Children* 1965 (fig.6), or the hawkish harlequin's squint in *Reflection (Self-Portrait)* 1981–2 (fig.39), suggest varieties of hauteur and the manufactured self. The conflicted and some-times vulnerable masculinities represented in some of Freud's self-portraits – but most especially his late ones – resemble the complex self-portraits of Lovis Corinth. Corinth's *Self-Portrait with a Glass* 1907, or *The Blinded Samson* 1909, both bear affinities with Freud's *Self-Portrait, Artist Working* (especially in terms of Corinth's increasingly informal finish after 1912). Similarly, the 'Man of Sorrows' element in Freud's *Painter Working, Reflection* 1993 (fig.13), acquires, by dint of the accumulation of extruded, broken surface paint as broken skin, a similarity with Corinth's 1920s painting *Ecce Homo*, which foregrounds a ragged paint version of skin as a means to signify the evidence of the Buffeting of Christ.

The disintegrating accumulation of skin, which was so central to William Sansom's abject novel of 1949, *The Body*, with its collection of discarded human membranes, was actualised by Freud in his paintings of bodies made in the 1990s. The historian of medical imaging, James Elkins, has discussed Freud's technique of using the broken and dragged skins of half-dried paint as close similes for the enduring and ageing skin of the

39
Reflection (Self-Portrait) 1981–2
Oil on canvas
55.9 × 50.8 (22 × 20)
Private Collection

40
Red Headed Man on a Chair
1962–3
Oil on canvas
91.5 × 91.5 (36 × 36)
Erich Sommer Holdings Ltd

human body.[25] These catastrophic residues of bulbs and flakes of paint invite comparison with the broken rashes of paint smeared across the raised surfaces of canvases by the artists whom Sickert called 'The Thickest Painters in London':[26] the Camden Town Neo-Realists, working on the threshold of The Great War – Harold Gilman and Charles Ginner. In the hands of Freud, could this real presence – the intrusive physicalities of the rough terrain of the paint-as-skin – be aligned to the rise of the new aesthetic of abjection in the art of the 1980s and after; that which Hal Foster has dubbed, 'The Return of the Real'?[27] Foster's 'Real' was based on Jacques Lacan's definition, a traumatic encounter that might make its way to the surface as a traumatic physical point, a knob of dead paint/skin, protruding in such a way that, 'we almost seem to touch the real'.[28] Also following Lacan, he connects this rising tear in the surface of representation with the gaze. This is reminiscent of the effect that emanates from *Painter Working, Reflection* (fig.13): a mixture of the uncanny agency of an implacable look and the traumatic surface; in Foster's words: '*It is as if this art wanted the gaze to shine, the object to stand, the real to exist . . . To this end it moves not only to attack the image but to tear at the screen, or to suggest that it is already torn.*'[29]

41
Lying by the Rags 1989–90
Oil on canvas
138.7 × 184.1 (54 5/8 × 72 1/2)
Astrup Fearnley Collection,
Oslo, Norway

The white rags with which Freud cleans his brushes after each stroke
become monuments in themselves to the *informe* and the abject; they
are first sighted like fallen clouds behind the *Red Headed Man on a Chair*
1962–3 (fig.40), becoming dirtied mountain ranges after 1986–7. They
are a sign of a surpassing of the boundary of clean/unclean that has been
accorded by Freud as near a sacramental condition as might be possible
in his world without transcendence; they are abject, but they are part
sublime. However, attempts to align the Freud of the 1980s and 1990s
with the emergence of a contemporary art focusing on abjection should,
of course, be qualified by Freud's emphatic commitment to Realism. He
suspends life in its physicality as paint/flesh. It is arrested, and the con-
tingent is preserved. Like Balthus stopping time, this arrest of the palpable
flesh in existence, where it serves to 'translate life into art', also arrests
the viewer's gaze amid the broken skins and flakes of paint. This virtually
transubstantiated world, like the Eucharistic paintings of Tintoretto in the
Scuola San Rocco in Venice, presents paint incorporating the carnal; it is
near-animate, and it bears with it the promise of Courbet – of a fantastic
merger of beholder and painted objects – 'a quasi-corporeal merger with
the subjects of his paintings'.[30]

Notes

FORMS OF SURVEILLANCE

1 Quoted in Catherine Lampert, *Lucian Freud/ Recent Work*, exh. cat., Whitechapel Art Gallery, London 1993, p.17.
2 Lucian Freud, 'Some Thoughts on Painting', *Encounter*, July 1954, p.23.
3 Sir John Rothenstein, *Modern English Painters*, vol. 3, London 1974, p.196.
4 Sigmund Freud, 'Three Essays on Sexuality', in James Strachey (ed.), *Standard Edition of the Complete Psychological; Works of Sigmund Freud*, vol. VII, 2001, London 1953, p.156.
5 Quoted in Lampert, op.cit., p.17.
6 Lucian Freud, *Cambridge Opinion*, no.37, p.47.
7 Ibid.
8 Quoted in Lampert, op.cit., p.17.
9 Lawrence Alloway, *Nine Abstract Artists*, London 1954, p.2.
10 In the Stendhalian sense, which Stephen Bann outlines in *The True Vine*, Cambridge 1989, p.171.
11 Ibid., p.168
12 Ibid., pp.169–70
13 Robert Hughes, *Lucian Freud Paintings*, London 1988, p.18.
14 William Sansom, *The Equilibriad*, London 1948, p.26.

WILD BODIES

1 William Sansom, *The Equilibriad*, London 1948, p.9.
2 Ibid. p.12.
3 See David Alan Mellor, 'Existentialism and British Art', in Francis Morris (ed.), *Paris Post War/ Art and Existentialism, 1945–55*, exh. cat., Tate Gallery, London 1993, pp.53–62.
4 Sansom, op.cit., pp.13, 17. The unlikely resemblance between Freud's illustrations and André Fougeron's paintings can be seen in examples such as Fougeron's *Hommage à Henri Houllier* (1949) (illus. *Paris/Paris . . .*, exh. cat., Centre Georges Pompidou, Paris 1981, p.211). When Freud arrived in Paris in Autumn 1946, he could well have seen the Fougeron exhibition at Galerie Billiet, which was held from 18 October to 16 November.

5 Sansom, op.cit. p.13; illustration facing p.26.
6 Ibid., p.17. In the text the boy stares at Paul for the duration of pages 16 to 19, while facing page 20 is Freud's illustration of this wide-eyed boy.
7 See David Sylvester, 'Un Parcours', in *Francis Bacon*, exh. cat., Centre Georges Pompidou, Paris 1996, p.20.
8 Peter Watson to John Craxton, c.August 1943, Craxton Archive, London.
9 See the definition in J. Laplanche and J-B Pontalis, *The Language of Psychoanalysis*, London 1973, pp.300–1.
10 The phrase 'Call to Order' designates the kind of monumental and Neo-classical figuration that flourished c.1916–25. In Britain, Cedric Morris, who had been Freud's teacher, was one of the key artists to transmit this style back from Paris.
11 Richard Calvocoressi, 'Introduction', in *Early Works/Lucian Freud*, exh. cat., Scottish National Museum of Modern Art, Edinburgh 1997, pp.14–15.
12 C.f. Eric J. Hosking and Cyril W. Newberry, *Birds of the Night*, London 1945.
13 This is reproduced in the animal almanac published in *The Saturday Book* in 1944; James Fisher, 'An Alphabet of Birds and Beasts', London 1943, pp.77–128.
14 One could compare this with the foetalised posture in the nudes of the 1980s and 1990s.
15 Linda Nochlin, 'Frayed Freud', *Artforum*, March 1994, pp.55–8.
16 Mikhail Bakhtin, *Rabelais and his World*, Indiana, Bloomington 1984, pp.353–4.
17 Mary Russo, *The Female Grotesque*, London 1995, p.28.
18 Catherine Lampert, *Lucian Freud*, exh. cat., Whitechapel Art Gallery, London 1993, p.23.
19 Russo, op.cit., p.24.
20 Ibid, p.29.
21 Illus. *Francis Gruber, 1912–1948*, Arts Council of Great Britain, London 1959, p.13. For Lampert's argument downplaying the possibility of Gruber's influence on Freud, see Lampert, op.cit., pp.14–15.

BRUTALIST ZONES

1 See Oswald Spengler, *The Decline of the West*, vol. II, London 1928, p.107.
2 Catherine Lampert, *Lucian Freud*, exh. cat., Whitechapel Art Gallery, London 1993, p.15.
3 Jacob Epstein to Peggy-Jean, 4 August 1954, Tate Archive 8716.33, quoted in Stephen Gardiner, *Jacob Epstein/Artist against the Establishment*, London 1992, p.451.
4 Lisa Tickner, *Modern Life and Modern Subjects/ British Art in the early 20th century*, London 2000, pp.307–8.
5 Lincoln Kirstein, *Quarry*, Pasedena, California 1986, p.107.
6 Ibid., p.63. Borstal Boys were male inmates of young offenders' detention centres. Freud personally knew at least one former Borstal Boy, the Irish playwright, Brenden Behan.
7 See the remarks on restoration in Suzanne Lowry, *The Young Fogey Handbook*, London 1985, pp.80–3.
8 Interview with Brian Kennedy, Director of the National Gallery of Australia, reported in the article 'Freud does serious sex', Features and Arts, smh.com, 28 May 2001, http://www.smh.com.au/news/0105/28/ features/features10.html.
9 Rose Macauley, *The World My Wilderness*, 1950, p.6.

MASQUERADES

1 See Francis Haskell, *History and its Images*, London 1993, p.220.
2 Sue Tilley, *Leigh Bowery/Life and Times of an Icon*, London 1997, p.220.
3 *Phenomena* was shown in London in 1938 and was critically condemned as a freak show. See also, Lincoln Kirstein, *Pavel Tchelitchew Drawings*, New York 1947, particularly the Runge-like illustration on p.43, as well as pp.44–46.
4 Leigh Bowery, 'Art and Love', *The Independent Magazine*, 11 January 1992.
5 See Freud's portraits of David Litvinoff: *The Procurer* (1954), and Harry Diamond: *Interior at Paddington* (1951).

6 Allon White, *Carnival, Hysteria and Writing*, London 1993, p.175.

7 'Leigh Bowery on Lucian Freud', in *Leigh Bowery*, London 1998, p.177.

8 See Hilton Als, in *Leigh Bowery*, London 1998, pp.111–5.

9 Sue Tilley, op.cit., p.220.

10 Mikhail Bakhtin, *Rabelais and his World*, Bloomington, Indiana 1984, p.300.

11 Helene Seckel, 'Three Portrait-Manifestos of Poets: André Salmon, Guillaume Apollinaire and Max Jacob', in William Rubin (ed.), *Picasso and Portraiture*, exh. cat., MOMA, New York 1996, p.189.

12 George T, Noszoply, 'Apollinaire, Allegorical Imagery and the Visual Arts', in Ian Higgins (ed.), *Literature and the Plastic Arts 1880–1930*, Edinburgh 1973, p.53.

13 For an account of these performances, see Tilley, op.cit., pp.216–8. Bowery was particularly interested in the Viennese Body artist Rudolf Schwarzkogler and the Aktionismus.

14 'It was the first time that many of the "club" people had been into an art gallery and it showed them what exciting places they can be.' Tilley, op.cit., p.218.

15 Roger Malbert, 'Exaggeration and Degradation: Grotesque Humour in Contemporary Art', in *Carnivalesque*, exh. cat., South Bank Centre/ National touring Exhibitions, London, p.90.

16 Nicholas Penny, 'The Early Works 1938–54', *Lucian Freud*, exh. cat., South Bank Centre, London 1988, p.7.

17 Harold Bloom, *The Anxiety of Influence*, London 1973, p.15.

18 Such as *Ein kind der Liebe*, reprinted in *Love above all and other drawings*, New York 1971, p.19.

19 Peter Sloterdijk, *Critique of Cynical Realism*, London 1988, p.410.

20 Reprinted as *Love above all and other Drawings*, op cit.

21 Lauter, op.cit., p.49.

22 Julia Kristeva, *Black Sun*, New York 1989, p.138.

23 Ibid., p.115.

SEEING A BODY OF PAINT

1 See the arguments of Maurice Merleau-Ponty, in amongst other essays, 'Eye and Mind', Galen A. Johnson (ed.), *The Merleau-Ponty Aestheticas Reader/Philosophy and Painting*, Illinois 1993, pp.121–149.

2 See some of the objectives enumerated by Paul Foss in his article, 'Eyes, Fetishism and the Gaze', *Art and Text*, no. 20, February – April 1986, pp.24–41.

3 For a focused account of the Mannheim exhibition and definitions of these terms, see Section 6, *Stationen der Moderne, Die bedeutenden Kunstausstellungen des 20. Jahrhunderts in Deutschland*, exh. cat., Berlinische Galerie, Berlin, 1988–9, pp.216–235.

4 Macauley, op.cit,. p.74.

5 Otto Dix, *Berliner Nachtausgabe*, 3 December 1927, reprinted, Charles Harrison and Paul Wood *Art in Theory 1900–1990*, Oxford and Cambridge, Mass 1992.

6 'La joie de l'amour arrete le temps ce qui est la seule eternité que l'homme ait jamais experimente', Georges Moulin, 'Ces Deux-La qui Vont Ensemble', *Cahier d'Art*, 1946, pp.200, 204.

7 'If you go to the flat, remember to look at the Picasso and Altdorfer books. Take them away if you would like to borrow them as I want you to see them.', Peter Watson, letter to John Craxton, undated, but c.1942, Craxton Archive, London.

8 See *Bruegel, une dynastie de peintres*, exh. cat., Palais des Beaux Arts, Brussels 1980, illus. no. 14.

9 'On Drawing', *Pavel Tchelitchew Drawings*, New York 1947, p.5.

10 See Stanley Kauffman, *Existentialism from Dostoevsky to Sartre*, New York 1956, p.13.

11 Fyodor Dostoyevsky, *The Idiot*, Harmondsworth 1955, p.216.

12 Ibid., p.225.

13 Ibid., p.210.

14 Julia Kristeva, *Black Sun*, New York 1989, p.113.

15 See Robert Bernasconi, 'One way Traffic: the Ontology of Decolonisation and its Ethics', and Michael B. Smith, 'Two Texts on Merleau-Ponty by Emmanuel Levinas', in Galen A. Johnson and Michael B. Smith (eds.), *Ontology and Alterity in Merleau Ponty*, Illinois 1990, pp.67–80; pp.53–66.

16 Emmanuel Levinas, *Otherwise Than Being*, Pittsburgh 1998, p.89.

17 Lawrence Gowing, *8 Figurative Painters*, New Haven 1981, p.15.

18 'But this experience (the encounter with Bacon) made him aware, as never before, of his need to represent volume.' Sir John Rothenstein, *Modern English Painters*, vol. 3, London 1974, p.197.

19 Cited in Catherine Lampert, *Lucian Freud/ Recent Work*, exh. cat., Whitechapel Art Gallery, London, 1993, p.17.

20 Michael Fried, *Courbet's Realism*, Chicago 1990.

21 Or from foot to paint: see the female painter with her toes on tubes of oils in *Painter and Model* (1986–7).

22 Lawrence Gowing, *Lucian Freud*, London 1982, pp.190–1, quoted in Michael Peppiatt, *A School of London/Six Figurative Painters*, exh. cat., British Council, London 1987, p.13.

23 Lucian Freud, 'Some thoughts on Painting', *Encounter*, July 1953, p.23.

24 Rolf Lauter, *Lucian Freud/Naked Portraits*, exh. cat., Museum für Moderne Kunst, Frankfurt am Main, 2000, p.94.

25 See James Elkins, *Pictures of the Body*, Stanford, California 1999, pp.57–9.

26 Walter Sickert, 'The Thickest Painters in London', *A Free House!*, London 1947, pp.183–6.

27 Hal Foster, *The Return of the Real*, London 1996, Chapter 3.

28 Ibid. p.134.

29 Ibid., pp.140–1, Foster's italics.

30 Anthony Bond, 'Embodying the Real', in *Body*, exh. cat., The Gallery of New South Wales, 1997, pp.11–80, p.24.

Index

Photographic Credits